BEI GRIN MACHT SICH IHR WISSEN BEZAHLT

AF141826

- Wir veröffentlichen Ihre Hausarbeit,
  Bachelor- und Masterarbeit

- Ihr eigenes eBook und Buch -
  weltweit in allen wichtigen Shops

- Verdienen Sie an jedem Verkauf

Jetzt bei www.GRIN.com hochladen und kostenlos publizieren

Mehmet Cosgun

How "helal" can an Islamic Bank be? The Islamic Finance in Germany and Turkey

Extracts of Dissertation

GRIN Verlag

Bibliografische Information der Deutschen Nationalbibliothek:

Die Deutsche Bibliothek verzeichnet diese Publikation in der Deutschen National-
bibliografie; detaillierte bibliografische Daten sind im Internet über http://dnb.d-
nb.de/ abrufbar.

Impressum:

Copyright © 2014 GRIN Verlag GmbH
Druck und Bindung: Books on Demand GmbH, Norderstedt Germany
ISBN: 978-3-656-68787-0

Dieses Buch bei GRIN:

http://www.grin.com/de/e-book/275683/how-helal-can-an-islamic-bank-be-the-
islamic-finance-in-germany-and

GRIN - Your knowledge has value

Der GRIN Verlag publiziert seit 1998 wissenschaftliche Arbeiten von Studenten, Hochschullehrern und anderen Akademikern als eBook und gedrucktes Buch. Die Verlagswebsite www.grin.com ist die ideale Plattform zur Veröffentlichung von Hausarbeiten, Abschlussarbeiten, wissenschaftlichen Aufsätzen, Dissertationen und Fachbüchern.

Besuchen Sie uns im Internet:

http://www.grin.com/

http://www.facebook.com/grincom

http://www.twitter.com/grin_com

MENDEL UNIVERSITY IN BRNO,

FACULTY OF BUSINESS AND ECONOMIC

THE ISLAMIC FINANCE – PUBLICATION DETAIL "HELAL":

HOW "HELAL" CAN AN ISLAMIC BANK BE?

EXTRACTS OF DISSERTATION

AUTHOR: MBA, MEHMET COSGUN

BRNO 2014

1. ABSTRACT

In a world of global finance, the cash flows are linked. So this applies also to the emerging Islamic financial institutions. Due to this background, I would like to dedicate myself to the important principle of Islamic finance, especially in Germany and Turkey.

The Islamic finance is an alternative to conventional finance. The Islamic finance is open to the whole humanity. By theirs sparing and careful action the Islamic finance could claim his market interest and need in the global economy since its founding's in the 1970's.

The world population exists to approximately 23% of Muslims. By Not-serving this population group by conventional bank houses and there special needs, further rising of Islamic finance houses becomes likely.

The economies in Islamic finance only allowed to trade and work with "halal" money. This means that the money from trade with forbidden substances is not "Helal". As practical examples mostly alcohol, pork etc. are listed.

But what is the concrete meaning of "Helal"? "Helal" means to be in line with ALLAH and his Kuran and to avoid "Haram" ways. The Islamic regulations gives corridors for which is economically spoken the frame for doing business. These "Helal"-frames are delivering corridors not only for economy, it is also valid for the Law regulation, society and government for a region, a nation, a continent and a global union?
For the better understanding and the implementing in my working of "Islamic Finance" it is crucial to use only my knowledge of Islam and deflecting it on my economic research.
The first critic; understands the pure regulations of "Helal" chained out of the Kuran, because understanding of this times descents and transforming on our current time and case is a highly responsible, complex topic.
The second critic; there is no complete "Helal" system implemented for all areas of Life. If we look on the field of Law, we found the most developed area so far, but in my personal view, we have even here negative movements, mostly titled with the term "shariah", which are leading humans on "Haram" ways.

I want to analyze the question of "helal" to pursue operational and real field experiences within finance world.

2. INTRODUCTION

My research work is motivated by clear and complementary knowledge between theoretical arguments and opinions in relation to Islamic finance.

This will be undertaken by comparison of a non-Muslim country such as Germany with a Muslim country such as Turkey.

There are, as in the Christian and Jewish world, many opinion leaders in the Islamic world. The publications display a consensus towards various theoretical objectives in an economic context. In most cases, however, there is little or no evidence base.

These publications display a use of old arguments, each side focused solely on the demand side or the supply side of economics.
Real challenges and developments may begin, from the author's perspective, only by practical, bottom up, analysis. The two essential components of the market were included in this study.

The problem that exists in the literature about facts and figures, for example, will be addressed through the creation of a separate factual basis.

The representative set of micro data will allow us to make a statistical interference, due to my work. This data is significant for a large number of people – for example, Muslims in Germany.

Furthermore, there is not a voice in the Muslim world, for example, defining the results of communication, benefits, advantages and disadvantages of Islamic finance, particularly in Germany or in Turkey.

The relevant questionnaire was distributed in an electronic form, with both residential and business customers involved. This result of the demand side has been reflected in workshops with banks.

The organization of this work is as follows. Initially, we started with an overview of research objectives. The research objectives are formulated into main objectives and secondary objectives (which are derived from the main objectives).

We are trying to get an idea of the demand for Islamic products looking to get market shares, even if the data is not readily available? (Visser, 2009)

2.1. QUESTIONS

If there is a demand for Islamic financial products, what are the indicators of choice? Are there Islamic financial products that only Muslims choose? What are the indicators of the distinction between Islamic and conventional banks?

In line with this background, I define the main objective of this thesis:

Is there a relationship between the number of Muslims in Germany and successful Islamic financial placement?

Derived Partial objectives

To achieve meaningful and differentiated models and measurable responses, we derive from the above target the following detailed issue positions. This method allows the author to achieve a quantitative and qualitative result range.

2.1.1.) Islamic finance institution, detail "Helal"
Can a "Helal" profit and loss participation system in a non-Muslim country be profitable and sustainable?
In an interview the relevant and important cornerstones are illuminated by "insiders".

3. METHODOLOGY

The leading objective of this research is to identify key market factors within the German market and, if necessary, by comparative with the Turkish market, in order to determine the relevance of Islamic finance. For this project, earlier empirical research results such as the IMF working paper from 2008 and empirical analysis from Islamic Banks regarding their financial stability are included.

A questionnaire distributed to private and business people has reached approximately 1,000 recipients in Germany. The responses include 73 from private individuals. The author has created a fact database with the feedback data from the electronic questionnaire. The first electronic distribution of the questionnaire did not receive satisfying return rates. In light of this, the interview form was chosen. This interview approach provided a substantially better answering rate and therefore a possible insight into the understanding of the external view has become possible. The demand indicators became available and their relevance to the definition of our problem has become clear. Our participants are engaged Muslims and mainly members in the Turkish, Islamic Organization DITIB.

In order to verify these outcomes, the author has provided the standard approach used in other areas. The choice of this approach was done openly, so that a legitimate statement to a gigantic number of people was possible. It was given in a political area, specifically one relation to classical elections.
Accordingly, an analogy has been chosen by "infratest Dimap", and we have found that the usual development of an "opinion picture" is usually done by a choice of 1,000 people as a controlling test for the German population of approximately 82 million human. If we now take our achieved comparative rate, this result gives us the impression that we can proceed to work with these results as usable.

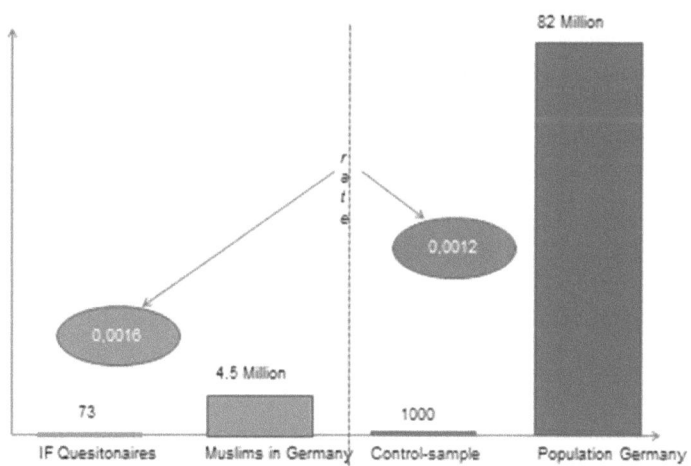

Figure 0: Results IF Questionnaire versus Rate (control-sample) Infratest-Dimap "Bundestagswahl" elections 2013
Source: Results IF Questionaire, Author

3.1 METHODS

The Islamic financial data are empirically tested in a survey. The necessary data generation was achieved using a standardized questionnaire. Results of the questionnaire are provided in section four; the questionnaire itself is attached in Appendix, Part 8.

3.2. LITERATURES

In this chapter, we will analyze the latest elaborations based on our questions in Chapter 2. We are starting with historical insights, and moving forward to the latest analyzes and publications.

Starting with the dissemination of the Kuran by an order from ALLAH to our Prophet Muhammad (s.a.v.), a well-known illiterate wholesaler, he was brought into knowledge of the other two main religions, Christianity and Judaism. This was necessary in order to fulfill the foundation of Islam as a whole. This inspiration has taken place around the existing knowledge; the main sources come from regional, cultural and human behavior at the time.

Looking at the economic dictates of the Kuran, we always find two essential conditions in several verses:

a) "Interest-free"
b) "Helal" (bypassing of "Haram")

Now, about 14 centuries later, we find that in many central banks such as the U.S. and Japan, the interest rate is at zero or only slightly above.

On July, 30th.2010, the three-month Libor was fixed at 0.46563 percent of dollar. Although not obviously unintentional, none of these countries has reduced its interest rate to zero for religious or ideological reasons. (Cizakca, 2011, p 230)

On the following pages, the findings are presented in clusters. Starting with the above-mentioned two main-conditions, they involve previously mentioned details, followed by market participants and the view of customers.

3.2.1. ISLAMIC FINANCE

Islamic economic theory and Islamic finance are in accordance with Islamic law. Economies may relate the application of Islamic law to economic activity; this applies to countries where Islamic rules are already in force, as well as not.

3.2.2. ISLAMIC ECONOMIC THOUGHTS

The early Muslim scholars have based their economic analyzes on the Kuran and the Sunnah, the sayings and doings of Prophet Muhammad (s.a.v.).This important transmitting of original sayings and doings is based on an excellent procedure for filtering the outcomes by sources and contents, over more than many centuries by selected personalities.

The most well-known Islamic scholar, who has written about the national economy, is *Ibn Khaldun (1332-1406)*, who is considered the father of modern economic theory.

Ibn Khaldun wrote on economically and politically relevant theories in his introduction to *"Mugadimah"* and in his *"Kitab al-Ilbar (History of the World)"*. In his books he talks about *"asabiyya" (social cohesion)*, which he developed as the cause of itself, to explain flourishing civilizations. Ibn Khaldun has found that many social forces behave cyclically, although there may be sudden, abrupt curves, which can break the overall development of a cycle.

3.2.3. CORNERSTONES OF ISLAMIC FINANCE

The basic tenets of Islamic finance are clearly set out in the following two verses of the Kuran:

Allah has carrion, blood, pork ... forbidden ... But who is forced, without exploitation and without exceeding ... there is no sin. Verily, Allah is Ever-Forgiving, Most Merciful. Kuran (172 ;)

Interest beneficiaries will rise up as the devil would have beaten them personally. This is for those who say, "Trade is like taking interest." But God has declared the trade "helal" and the rate and any type of it as "haram"... Kuran (274)

The first verse (172) explains that certain offenses in certain circumstances can be tolerated. To this end, Muslims must be included, even when in so-called non-Muslim countries. Where focus is intense, there is always a permanent Muslim motivation for obtaining the fully comprehensive union with the Kuran.

The second verse (274) stipulates that an Islamic financial system must be based on trade and production, and only prohibits interest. It defines that the financial products have to be "Helal" and have to follow the principles by avoiding "Haram" bids. A core principle is that Islamic finance is an equity-based system, where all financial agreements are based on profit and loss sharing of the economic results. All financial assets are dependent claims, and there are no debt securities with fixed or revolving interest rates.

3.2.4. ISLAMIC FINANCE, DETAIL HELAL

That several Islamic financial institutions are already operating successfully for several years in other nations, such as the UK, adds to our research a differentiated view regarding the characteristics of German market.

With a Muslim population of more than 4 million people, and with significant direct investment in comprehensive and economic relations with the world, Germany could be an interesting location for an Islamic bank? (Naggar, 1984 in Khan and Porzio, 2010).

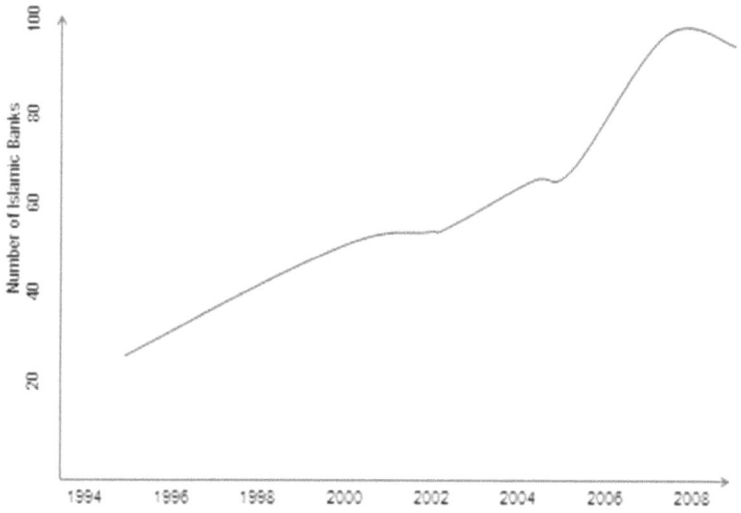

Figure 3: Number of Islamic Banks reporting to Database Bankscope 1995 - 2008.
Source: World-Bank Report, October 2010, Thorsten Beck, Asli Demirgüç-Kunt, Ouarda Merrouche

4. RESULTS, DETAIL HELAL

As another point he observes is demand as critical. Of course, this subject has been already discussed internally. When in dialogue the "Helal" subject was demanded, here it has been looked at by reference to the legislative situation in Germany. Beside this, there are strong, regional differences within Germany. This means that in one federal state functions can fail in a different federal state. If one looks at this subject from the internal point of Isbank, we have to say that there is no discernible demand for islamic financial products so far. This can be observes by the fact that if somebody looks for Islamic financial products, they do not necessarily come first to the Isbank; perhaps, rather to the Kuveyt Türk.

Figure 14: the structure of an Islamic bank is founded with the deposit accounts for each investor. At the second level, the "clearing/ ruling" accounts are handling money, which contents interest, e.g. money for refinancing from the central banks. The "participation" is the Islamic achievements basin, e.g. a joint venture is delivering a loss or profit, and at the last level the investments or profits of e.g. joint ventures are transformed into stocks.

Account Structure of Islamic Banks, example Kuveyt Türk

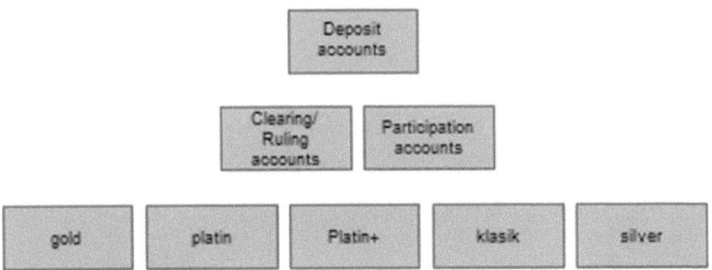

Figure 14: Results "interest Free Bank".
Source: internal Data Kuveyt Turk,
Economic Conferences, Brno, Author, 7./8. March 2013

Differences between Islamic Finance and Conventional Banking in daily Business

The best known rule is the difference that an Islamic bank must work "interest-free". To understand the concept "interest-free", we must explain the difference between the automatic one and the fixed extra charge. The amount of the interest is not vital whether it is a little or a lot. The meaning of interest: if somebody lends money, and the original amount finds an automatic increase without any risk, this is called interest. However, trade requires that, for example, somebody effects a purchase for 1 piece of gold of a product and sells it for, for example, a 1.10 piece of gold. In this action no automatism of the monetary rise is included, an enterprise risk and the possibility of a loss is given. In our example it is also possible that the market will deliver just a price of 0.90 pieces of gold.

As for conventional banks like Deutsche Bank, HSBC and Isbank, the biggest scope of business has been reached by grants of credit with interests; these grants of credit take place directly between the bank and the customer.

Islamic banks lead their main businesses in a triangular nature. The bank, the customer and a real product or a service are the conditions for this. The bank purchases the service or the product and resells ahead to the final customer with a fixed extra charge. These conditions are discussed before completion of the financial transaction and are fixed in an agreement.

Figure 16: Here the complete range of Islamic banking products is mentioned, the possible agreements of a financial transaction. The main cluster are Sales with a fixed extra charge, Joint ventures, Leasings and Services

Islamic Banking Products

Finance / Sales	Leasings	Services, including fixed fees
• Sarf (spot)	• Ijara (services and use of assets, equipment's, office automation etc.)	• Wakala (power of attorney)
• Murabaha (trading)		• Kafalah (guarantees)
• Salam (options)	• Ijara Thumma Al-Bai (services, use and followed by purchasing option of assets, equipment's etc.)	• Hiwala (money transfers)
• Istisna (paid product by bank, which will be produced later and distributed to agreed final user)		
• Bay' Bithaman 'Ajil (deferred payment sale)	**JointVentures**	
• Bay al 'Inah (sale and buy-back agreement)	• Mudaraba (money based investments of partners)	
• Tawarruq (commodity business by involving firstly the bank, before selling it to customer liquidity keeping procedure)	• Musharaka (one side money, other side management and work)	
• Arbun (deposits)		

Figure 16: Results "helal" Banking, Source: internal Data Kuveyt Turk, Economic Conferences, Brno, Author, 7./8. March 2013

11

Main Product Portfolio of Kuveyt Türk

-> Murabaha –   Tradings with e.g. commodities and selling with an fixed fee
to final customers

-> Mudaraba –   JointVentures; one site putting cash in, the other site the
Management and work

-> Musarake –   Joint Ventures, both sites putting cash in the project

-> Icare –   Leasing/ Rent businesses

Real Economy

Figure 17: Results "interest Free Bank",
Source: internal Data Kuveyt Turk,
Economic Conferences, Brno, Author, 7./8. March 2013

Serving Customer Needs with an Islamic Bank, in Turkey
The Islamic banks in Turkey are registered to the central regulations and
established like the other 5.411 conventional banks. Therefore they are like at
any other bank, with the account opening the insert protection through the state
having been activated and guaranteed.
All bank products of modern finance are also offered by Islamic banks.
Moreover, products are purchased in advance and will transfer rates to the
customer. Also, leasing is possible.
The products and services which are not "helal" in Islam are excluded of course.
In Islamic finance all activities are linked to a real, present product or service.
Instead of the conventional loan business, the profit and loss participation
construct is carried out. The Islamic principles are the basic construction of an
Islamic bank. The Islamic banks are currently integrating every regional
legislation and default.

Account forms:

a)   Regulation cash discount (mevzuat hesap)
     b)   1) special Middle account, (cari hesap) Cleaning
          2) Participation cash discount, (katilim hesap)
               c)   Property: gold, platinum, silver

Special middle accounts:
On these accounts, Turkish lira and/or foreign currencies are put down in a "washbasin", this money contains interest and therefore it is not compatible with Islamic principles, and is therefore separated from the core business. Examples for this include: change fees in interest forms, credit cards fees in forms similar to interest etc.
This action is necessary to generate "avoidable" disadvantages in the global business. The aim of the main business remains and the financial products are like, for example, mudabarah.

Participation accounts
On these accounts the Islamic working capital is deposited in Turkish lira and/or foreign currencies in the fund. The strict separation between the Islamic working capital and the middle accounts is firmly supervised.

Property, like platinum, silver and gold, are acceptable precious metal deposits.

5. DISCUSSION, DETAIL "HELAL"

A further, aggregated cornerstone of Islamic Finance is titled with the "helal" regulatory, which is explaining to do careful business in line with the rules of Islam. In Front of this background, we find regulation authorities in the German market, which obviously are not too familiar with the Islamic finance concepts. The officially mentioned doubts are in regard of insert protection, investments and the operational usage of Profit- and Loss Sharing System. Mr. Naggar asked already in 1984 the question, why no Islamic Finance institution is established in Germany. *(Naggar, 1984 in Porzio, Khan, 2010)*

We combine this finding with Beck, Demirgüc-Kunt and Merrouche, which delivered the increasing number of Islamic Banks starting reporting to the database BankScope. In this context we see even Great Britain with two fully working Islamic banks. *(Beck, Demirgüc-Kunt, Merrouche, 2010)*

With Nienhaus, we understand that Islamic countries have start developing this Islamic economic model, while understanding the disadvantages of capitalism and socialism since the last decades, and that this process is still working. *(Nienhaus, 2010)*

We have to take into our consideration that the legal situation in Germany is the reason for the currently situation of no Islamic Bank. This is quite interesting in a European Market with the example of e.g. Great Britain. The further doubt is that if one Islamic Bank has one license in one EU member country, this is valid for the whole EU.
Mr. Mahlknecht showed us impressively in detail how a non-Muslim market can successfully integrate the Islamic financial important nuances into the own market. *(Mahlknecht, 2008)*

The products, separated accounting and the tri-angle System showed how the main objective of a typical Islamic Bank is working. We see the examples in British and Turkish markets, which are originally conventional banking markets and the success of Islamic banks, including the full insert protection of customers. Herewith we learned that all common Finance products can be offered by Islamic Banks.
In the opposite direction and further analyze we see also originally conventional founded Banks like Deutsche Bank and HSBC working in typical and exclusively Islamic Banking markets.

Summary
If we see the current living and successful model of Islamic financial Institutions in non-Muslim countries, we have to note that there are -for the author not reproducible-, seems like mainly political motivated restrictions especially in Germany. We find here an obvious lack of information and knowledge, which are leading regulation institutions for not licensing and enabling the entry of Islamic Banks.

We have learned that this approach has to be done better on a European level and the need of consequently harmonizing this regulation operational within the European market.

It is heavily critical, accepting situations in Europe, in which one of the foundation pillars of the Union like "free and liberal trade within the union" is handled so much differentiated, as we learned in our research for Islamic finance.

6. SUMMARY, DETAIL "HELAL"

Islamic finance institution, detail "Helal"
We asked: Can a profit and loss participation system in a non-Muslim country, be "Helal" profitable and sustainable?
Here again, we verified that it is possible to work as an Islamic Bank profitable and sustainable in a non-Muslim country.

Recommendations
We want to remember the developments of Islamic Finance started in the last decades. The basic motivation is to establish an Islamic way beside the main concepts of capitalism and socialism. In both of these cases we have learned the advantages and disadvantages of the systems. The motivations behind these concepts are the key difference. Mr. Keynes highlighted his findings in 1936 and we showed the motives in chapter 3. Viewed by the Islamic "helal" rules, we found that except the motivation "greed" and "enjoying interest", the financial behavior of Muslims are similar. *(Keynes, 1936)*

In our research we get the impression, that regulation authorities especially in Germany has some lack in understanding the cornerstones of e.g. "helal" concepts. Focusing on the insert protection, the Supervisory Board Council of an Islamic Bank and the Profit and Loss Sharing System are most critical in their understanding.

For this purpose we like to concentrate on the situation of debt overloaded private households in e.g. Germany and the actual behavior of conventional financial institutions. If the loan rate for let us say the housing is not been paid in exact time, the ruling of banks are allowing to add extra interest charges for this "default" behavior.

After the usual reception of delayed money transfers, the bank is transmitting primarily the portion for serving the interest rate and the extra interest charge, before transmitting and clearing the primary debt. The effect is clear in regard of the primary debt with lower decreasing movements and higher direct proportionate interest rate.

It is worth thinking about the further effects of this quite small detail, which is absolutely in line with financial regulations authorities BaFin and BaKred.

Suggests
For reviewing this aspect and avoiding falsifications in this context, it would be a good analyze to see the interest business in e.g. Europe, divided through the normal, agreed contractual interest business and the various kinds of penalty interests currently with all participants in the process.

7. References

BECK, DEMIRGÜC-KUNT, MERROUCHE, 2010, "Islamic vs. Conventional Banking", Policy Research Paper 5446, World Bank.

CIHAK, MARTIN AND HESSE, HEIKO 2008, "Islamic Banks and Financial Stability: An Empirical Analysis," IMF Working Paper WP/08/16, Washington, DC: IMF.

CIZAKCA, MURAT, 2011, "Islamic Capitalism and Finance", Edward Elgar, ISBN 978 0 85793 147 4.

KHALDUN, IBN, 1332-1406, "Mugadimah", "Kitab al-Ilbar"

KEYNES, J.M., 1936, "General Theory of Employment, Interest and Money", New York.

KHAN, M. FAHIM AND PORZIO, MARIO, 2010, "Islamic Banking and Finance in the European Union", Edward Elgar, ISBN 978 1 94980 017 4.

MAHLKNECHT, MICHAEL, 2009, "Islamic Finance, Einführung in Theorie und Praxis", Wiley Verlag, ISBN 978-3-527-50389-6.

NIENHAUS, VOLKER, KAS REPORTS, 2010

VISSER, HANS, 2009, "Islamic Finance, Principles and Practice", Edward Elgar, ISBN 978 1 84542 525 8.

8. Appendix

Questionnaire

Please answer questions step by step!

A) Private Clients :

2   Age
3   Place of Birth
4   Male/ Female
5   Married
6   Children
7   Education
8   Profession
9   Believe:
10 Your Interest in assets including Values
11 Own land   100% scale detail related total
12 Own appartement
13 Own house
14 Credit
15 Shortterm
16 Longterm
17 Debit
18 Shortterm
19 Longterm
20 Others: if yes specify
21 Financial and banking products
22 Insurances (list of most common insurances, incl. Housesaving)
23 (Clustering important structural common items, if necessary -> Islamic Law allowance?)
24 Housesaving Contract (Bausparvertrag)
25 Shortterm credit (Dispositionkredit)
26 Value and Interest rate
27 Longterm credit (Darlehen, privat und geschäftlich)
28 Value and Interestrate
29 Shortterm credit
30 Value and Interest rate
31 Longterm credit
32 Value and Interest rate
33 Shares
34 Value and Interest rate
35 Bonds
36 Value and Interest rate?
37 Options
38 Value and Interest rate?
39 Satisfied?
40 Demand Rate?
41 What is the negative effect of before mentioned products in your opinion?
42 Verify so far expectations, feeling?
43 What is the best effect of before mentioned products in your opinion?
44 Verify your expectations also, for later suggestions part important?
45 What is your opinion or/and knowledge about Islamic financial or/ and banking products?
46 Current available Islamic financial products you know
47 Insurances house saving
48 Fixed fee rates for credits
49 Else:
50 Interest, demand rate
51 Name of Bank?
52 Value of Assets?
53 Value of Credits?

54 **Possible available Islamic financial products:**
55 Suggestion of all financial/ insurance products in line with Islamic rules?
56 Name of Bank ?
57 Possible Value of Assets?
58 Possible Value of Credits?
59 Interest, demand rate
60 **Advantage conventional banking**
61 **Disadvantage conventional banking**
62 **Advantage Islamic banking**
63 **Disadvantage Islamic banking**

64 B) Business Clients :

65 Age
66 Place of Birth
67 Male/ Female
68 Married
69 Children
70 Education
71 Profession
72 Believe:
73 **Position in Market**
74 _Established year
75 Staff
76 Market (regional)   National   Europe   World
77 **Universal bank**
78 **Specific bank**
79 **Financial and banking products portfolio**
80 Insurances (list of most common insurances, incl. Housesaving)
81 (Clustering important structural common items, if necessary -> Islamic Law allowance?)
82 Housesaving Contract (Bausparvertrag)
83 Shortterm credit (Dispositionkredit)
84 Value and Interest rate
85 Longterm credit (Darlehen, privat und geschäftlich)
86 Value and Interestrate
87 Shortterm credit
88 Value and Interest rate
89 Longterm credit
90 Value and Interest rate
91 Shares
92 Value and Interest rate
93 Bonds
94 Value and Interest rate?
95 Options
96 Value and Interest rate?
97 Satisfied?
98 Demand Rate?
99 What is the negative effect of before mentioned products in your opinion?
100 Verify so far expectations, feeling?
101 What is the best effect of before mentioned products in your opinion?
102 Verify your expectations also, for later suggestions part important?
103 What is your opinion or/and knowledge about Islamic financial or/ and banking products?
104 **Current available Islamic financial products**
105 Insurances house saving
106 Fixed fee rates for credits
107 Else:
108 Interest, demand rate
109 Name of Bank?
110 Value of Assets?
111 Value of Credits?
112 **Possible available Islamic financial products portfolio:**

113 Bai' al 'inah (sale and buy-back agreement)
114 Bai' bithaman ajil (deferred payment sale)

115 Bai' muajjal (credit sale)
116 Musharakah
117 Mudarabah
118 Bai salam
119 Musawamah
120 Ijarah
121 Advantages of Ijarah
122 Hibah (gift)
123 Ijarah thumma al bai' (hire purchase)
124 Ijarah-wal-iqtina
125 Qard hassan/ Qardul hassan (good loan/benevolent loan)
126 Sukuk (Islamic bonds)
127 Takaful (Islamic insurance)
128 Wadiah (safekeeping)
129 Islamic equity funds
130 Wakalah (power of attorney)

131 **Advantage conventional banking clients**
132 **Disadvantage conventional banking clients**
133 **Advantage Islamic banking clients**
134 **Disadvantage Islamic banking clients**